WORLD SERIES CHAMPIONS

MINNESOTA TWINS

Published by Creative Education
P.O. Box 227, Mankato, Minnesota 56002
Creative Education is an imprint of The Creative Company
www.thecreativecompany.us

Design and production by Blue Design
Printed in the United States of America

Photographs by Corbis (Bettmann, Bettmann/CORBIS, Minnesota Historial Society, Brian
Snyder/Reuters), Getty Images (Diamond Images, Stephen Dunn, Focus on Sport, Otto Greule
Jr, Judy Griesedieck//Time Life Pictures, Robert Leiter/MLB Photos, MLB Photos, National
Baseball Hall of Fame Library/MLB Photos, Anthony Neste//Time Life Pictures, Tom Pidgeon,
Rich Pilling/MLB Photos, Bill Polo/MLB Photos, Louis Requena/MLB Photos, Ryan/Beyer,
Herb Scharfman/Sports Imagery, Gregory Shamus, Jon SooHoo/MLB Photos, Tony Tomsic/
MLB Photos, Ron Vesely/MLB Photos, Hank Walker//Time Life Pictures, John Willimason/MLB
Photos, Alex Wong, Michael Zagaris/MLB Photos)

Library of Congress Cataloging-in-Publication Data

Frisch, Aaron.
Minnesota Twins / by Aaron Frisch.
p. cm. — (World Series champions)
Includes index.
ISBN 978-1-58341-695-2
1. Minnesota Twins (Baseball team)—History—Juvenile literature. I. Frisch, Aaron, 1975- History
of the Minnesota Twins. II. Title. III. Series.

GV875.M55F75 2009
796.357'6409776579—dc22   2008003767

First edition
9 8 7 6 5 4 3 2 1

Cover: Pitcher Francisco Liriano (top), third baseman Harmon Killebrew (bottom)
Page 1: Pitcher Johan Santana
Page 3: Catcher Joe Mauer

MINNESOTA TWINS

AARON FRISCH

CREATIVE EDUCATION

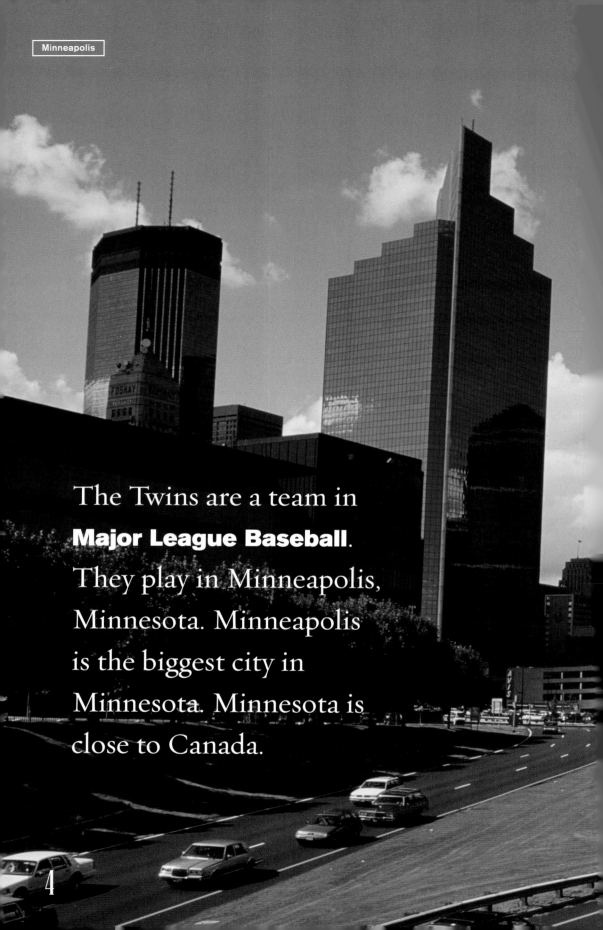

The Twins are a team in **Major League Baseball**. They play in Minneapolis, Minnesota. Minneapolis is the biggest city in Minnesota. Minnesota is close to Canada.

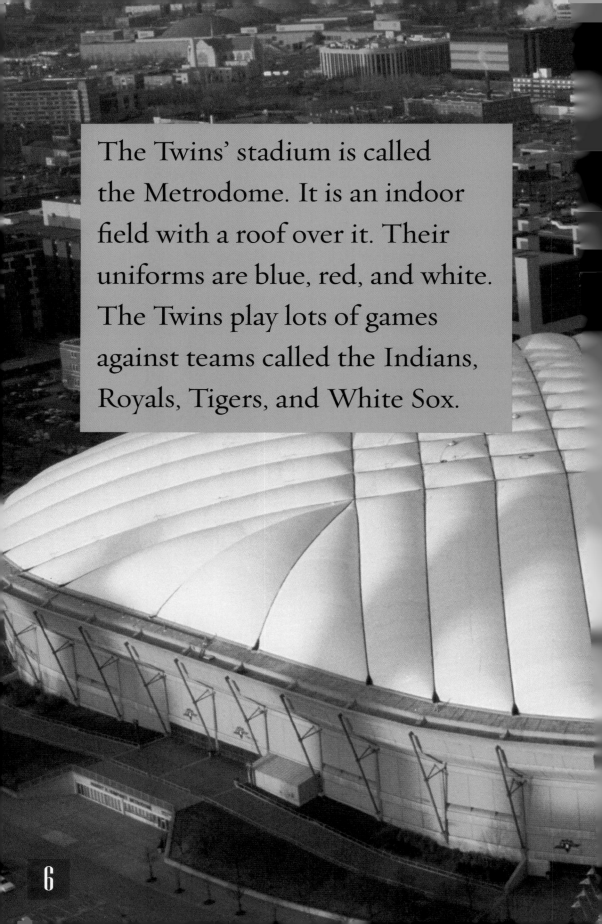

The Twins' stadium is called the Metrodome. It is an indoor field with a roof over it. Their uniforms are blue, red, and white. The Twins play lots of games against teams called the Indians, Royals, Tigers, and White Sox.

Metrodome

7

WALTER JOHNSON

Catcher Earl Battey

The Twins started out as a team called the Senators in 1901. The Senators played in Washington, D.C. They won the World Series in 1924. But the Senators were not very good after that. In 1961, they moved to Minnesota and became the Twins.

THIRD BASEMAN
HARMON KILLEBREW

Outfielder Tony Oliva

The Twins were a good team in the 1960s. Third baseman Harmon Killebrew hit lots of home runs. He helped the Twins get to the World Series in 1965. But they lost. Second baseman Rod Carew (*cuh-ROO*) helped the Twins make the **playoffs** two times after that.

11

Second baseman Rod Carew

Bert Blyleven was a star pitcher for the Twins in the 1970s. He liked throwing **curveballs**. But the Twins were not as good anymore.

WORLD SERIES CHAMPIONS
MINNESOTA TWINS

BERT BLYLEVEN

OUTFIELDER
KIRBY PUCKETT

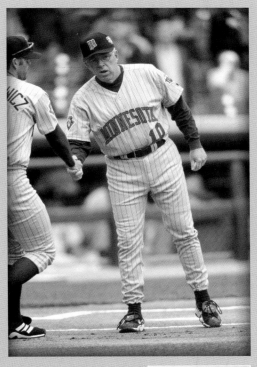
Manager Tom Kelly

In 1984, the Twins got a new outfielder named Kirby Puckett. He was a good hitter and played hard on defense. The Twins got a smart manager named Tom Kelly, too.

OUTFIELDER
CHILI DAVIS

17

First baseman Kent Hrbek

Puckett helped the Twins get
to the World Series in 1987.
They beat a team called the
Cardinals to win their first world
championship. The Twins won
another World Series in 1991!

THIRD BASEMAN
GARY GAETTI

19

Pitcher Johan Santana

The Twins had some bad seasons after that. But they got to the playoffs many times starting in 2002. Outfielder Torii (*TO-ree*) Hunter made lots of exciting catches. Pitcher Johan (*YO-hon*) Santana struck out batters with his **changeup** pitches.

OUTFIELDER
TORII HUNTER

21

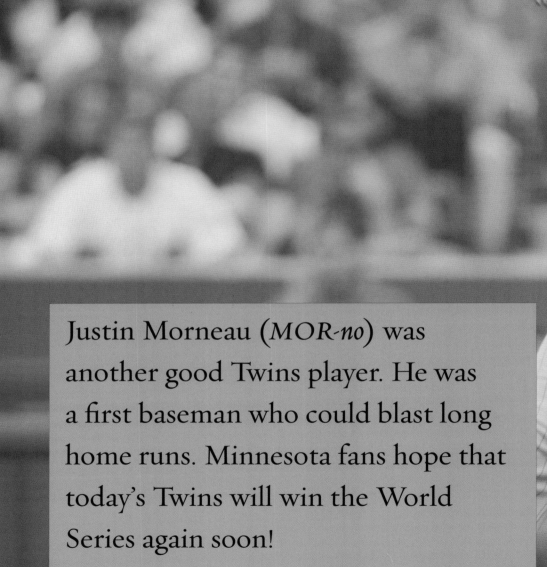

Justin Morneau (*MOR-no*) was another good Twins player. He was a first baseman who could blast long home runs. Minnesota fans hope that today's Twins will win the World Series again soon!

FIRST BASEMAN
JUSTIN MORNEAU

GLOSSARY

changeup — a pitch that tricks batters because it looks like a fastball but goes slower

curveballs — pitches that spin the ball and make it curve down

Major League Baseball — a group of 30 baseball teams that play against each other; major-league teams have the best players in the world

playoffs — games that are played after the season to see which team is the champion

TWINS FACTS

Team colors: blue, red, and white

First home stadium (in Minnesota): Metropolitan Stadium

Home stadium today: Hubert H. Humphrey Metrodome

League/Division: American League, Central Division

First season in Minnesota: 1961

World Series championships: 1987, 1991

Team name: The Twins got their name because they play in Minneapolis. Minneapolis is right next to a city called St. Paul. People call Minneapolis and St. Paul the "Twin Cities."

Major League Baseball Web site for kids:
http://www.mlb.com/mlb/kids/

INDEX